INCREDIBLE INSECTS

GRASSHOPPERS

James E. Gerholdt

Published by Abdo & Daughters, 4940 Viking Drive, Suite 622, Edina, Minnesota 55435.

Printed in the United States.

Cover Photo credit: Peter Arnold, Inc.
Interior Photo credits: James Gerholdt, pages 5, 7, 11
                        Peter Arnold, pages 9, 13, 15, 17, 19, 21

Edited by Julie Berg

Library of Congress Cataloging-in-Publication Data

Gerholdt, James E., 1943
    Grasshoppers / James E. Gerholdt.
    p. cm. — (Incredible insects)
Includes index.
ISBN 1-56239-485-1
1. Grasshoppers—Juvenile literature. [1. Grasshoppers.] I. Series:
Gerholdt, James E., 1943- Incredible insects.
QL508.A2G35 1995
595.7'26--dc20   95-7581
                                               CIP
                                               AC

Contents

GRASSHOPPERS

Grasshoppers belong to one of the 28 insect orders. Locusts and katydids are grasshopper types. Crickets also belong to this order.

Insects are arthropods. This means their skeleton is on the outside of their body. They also are ectothermic—they get their body temperature from the environment.

There are over 20,000 species in this order, about 15,000 of which are grasshoppers. They are found worldwide, wherever it is not too cold.

Grasshoppers usually have four wings, hindlegs that are made for jumping, a mouth that can chew, and antennae that can be short or very long.

Right:
The southeastern lubber grasshopper has short antennae and a mouth that can chew.

LIFE CYCLE

All grasshoppers go through a simple metamorphosis. This means they hatch from an egg and spend the first part of their life as a nymph. The eggs are laid in the ground or sometimes in plants. Some species lay their eggs one by one, while others lay them in batches of 10 to 200.

A female grasshopper has an ovipositor that digs into the soil or plant so the eggs are safe from enemies. After the nymphs hatch, they may shed their skin three to five times before they become adults.

**Right:
Eggs from a
spur-throated
grasshopper
found in the
eastern United
States.**

SIZES

Grasshoppers are medium to large-sized insects. But a few species are small. The pygmy grasshoppers only reach a length of 3/4 of an inch (19 mm). Other species may only grow to less than 1/2 of an inch (13 mm) long.

The angular winged katydid can be 2 1/4 inches (57 mm) long. The largest of all the grasshoppers can grow 6 inches (15 cm) long. Another species, the band-winged grasshopper, grows to 1 1/4 inches (32 mm) long. All grasshopper wings are usually twice as wide as the body is long.

**Right:
The lubber
grasshopper
nymph.**

SHAPES

Most of the grasshoppers are long and slender, with long hindlegs. One of the South American species is so long and slender it looks like a stick!

Some katydids are short and fat. Their bodies are almost as high as they are long. The front wings are narrow and hard. They protect the hindwings which are wide and fold like a fan.

Some species, like the katydids, have antennae longer than their bodies. Others, like the short-horned grasshoppers, have very short antennae.

All grasshoppers have three body parts: the head, thorax, and abdomen. They also have six legs and a pair of antennae.

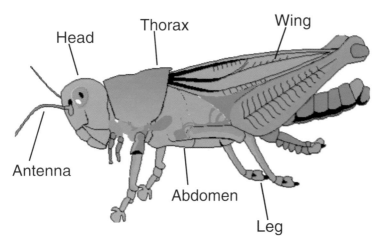

Head
Thorax
Wing
Antenna
Abdomen
Leg

**Right:
This southeastern
lubber grasshopper
has long, slender
hindlegs.**

COLORS

Grasshoppers are usually brown or tan. Katydids are often a very bright shade of green, or sometimes a bright yellow. But no matter what shade they are, they blend in with their environment. This is called camouflage.

A bright green katydid on a bright green leaf is difficult to see. A dull brown grasshopper would blend into the ground easily. Some species are colored the same as dead twigs and leaves.

Although the grasshoppers' bodies are not very colorful, their wings often are. These colors only show when the grasshoppers are flying. Some species have bright red or green wings.

**Right:
The rainbow
grasshopper is very
colorful. It is found in
the desert grassland
of Arizona.**

13

WHERE THEY LIVE

Grasshoppers are found in many different habitats. Some species burrow into the soil or rotten wood. Other species live in fields, deserts, gardens, or in trees around houses.

Other grasshoppers live in the jungle or the rain forest. Here, many different species are found, each having their own special place in the environment.

Since the nymphs have no wings, they stay in the same area. The adults often fly from place to place.

**Right:
Some grasshoppers
live in sand.**

SENSES

Grasshoppers have the same five senses as humans. Their eyesight is very good. This helps them find food and watch for enemies.

Hearing is another important sense. The males create a loud "song" by rubbing either the front wings or the hindlegs together. This "song" attracts females and keeps other males away. The grasshoppers' ears are on the abdomen or legs.

**Right:
The grasshopper's
eyesight helps it
find food.**

DEFENSE

Camouflage is the grasshoppers' best defense against enemies. Despite their habitat or color, grasshoppers can be difficult to see. They also jump or fly to escape enemies.

The bright wing colors can distract an enemy. And if they fold their wings in flight and land, they just seem to disappear!

Grasshoppers also taste bad. Even more, they can spit up their food, called "tobacco juice," to defend themselves. And they can break off their hindleg, if needed, to make an escape from enemies!

**Right:
The body of the leaf
katydid resembles
the green leaves on
which it lives.**

FOOD

Grasshoppers are usually plant-eaters. Some grasshoppers, like locusts, destroy crops. A swarm of locusts can destroy entire fields.

Unusual amounts of rain can create plenty of food for the locusts to eat. The more they eat, the more they reproduce. Soon a swarm is created. A large swarm may contain 50,000 million locusts that, when in flight, can block out the sun!

Right:
Locusts can be very
destructive to plants.

GLOSSARY

Abdomen (AB-do-men) - The rear body part of an arthropod.

Antennae (an-TEN-eye) - A pair of sense organs found on the head of an insect.

Arthropod (ARTH-row-pod) - An animal with its skeleton on the outside of its body.

Camouflage (CAM-a-flaj) - The ability to blend in with the surroundings.

Ectothermic (ek-toe-THERM-ik) - Regulating body temperature from an outside source.

Environment (en-VI-ron-ment) - Surroundings in which an animal lives.

Habitat (HAB-uh-tat) - An area in which an animal lives.

Insect (IN-sekt) - An arthropod with three body parts and six legs.

Metamorphosis (met-a-MORF-oh-sis) - The change from an egg to an adult.

Nymph (NIMF) - The young of an insect that goes through a simple, or incomplete metamorphosis.

Order (OAR-der) - A grouping of animals.

Ovipositor (o-vee-POS-i-tore) - A long, tube-like body part that a female grasshopper uses to lay her eggs.

Species (SPEE-seas) - A kind or type.

Swarm (SWORM) - A large number of insects moving from one place to another.

Thorax (THORE-axe) - The middle body part of an arthropod.

INDEX

About the Author

Jim Gerholdt has been studying reptiles and amphibians for more than 40 years. He has presented lectures and displays throughout the state of Minnesota for nine years. He is a founding member of the Minnesota Herpetological Society and is active in conservation issues involving reptiles and amphibians in India, Aruba, and Minnesota.

Photo by Tim Judy